CHRISTOPHER FONTES

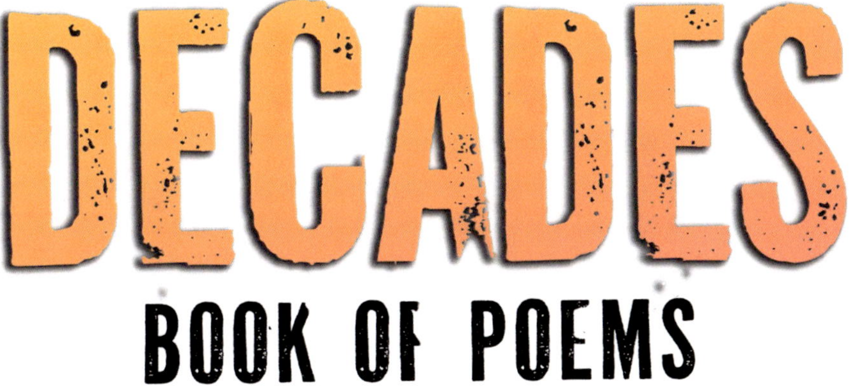

BOOK OF POEMS

POETIC EXPRESSIONS PRESENTS, LLC

CONTENTS

WHAT IS DECADES: BOOK OF POEMS?

Decades is a collection of poems that were inspired by songs that I have listened to and gained inspiration from. This collection of poems are reminiscent of songs you may or may not have heard. The goal was to capture the essence of appreciation and inspiration all in one. I hope my words written evoke thought, perspective and understanding through poetic expressions.

As an artist we all gain inspiration from a variety of things, "Decades" is my initial showcase of inspiration. As you read the poems written, grasp the appreciation for the original concept and feel the evolution of thought throughout. I used to make mixtapes back in Highschool. In doing so, I learned how to put a playlist together with a group of songs that I liked on one project. Now I get to do so with my own project!

"Decades: Mixtape of Poems" Is a unique mix of poems that captures and highlights the essence of inspiration of the poems throughout. Poetry to me, is my most profound form of communication. I create and formulate concepts creatively in a way that doesn't always flow as naturally when not in creator mode. Whether You listen to the Spoken Word, read the poems, or pair the two together. Be inspired, vibe out, and most of all, allow the poetry to resonate with you and inspire what it naturally inspires within you.

DECADES:

MIXTAPE OF POEMS

THE SIGHT OF HER BEAUTY IS ENOUGH TO LEAVE ME SPEECHLESS

Put on your red dress, and

Slip on your high heels. Please forgive

These hands of mine. Their just appreciating the

Way those thighs feel. I believe your

Looking your best. It's making me

Want you more, but then again

I never took you for less. Tonight's

One of those nights you shouldn't

Be looking for rest. Tonight's one

Of those nights you should be looking

For sex. Better yet let's make love. What I

Wanna do to you, is every single thing that

I can Think of. Lay you down and caress you

I'll lick, but if I drown promise you'll cum for

My rescue. I'm here to highlight how beautiful

You look. I'm also here to undress you.

Intense moments filled with intensity.

Easy to say, easy to feel like I don't know

What got into me. But the truth is I do, it's you

And the way you look, I mean whoo! I mean

Damn. I mean it wouldn't be me if I

Didn't do what I do, plus you know who

I am. Tonight you'll know me much better.

What if I told you, your clothing's like feathers?

And by that I meant, that its adorning.

Warning every signal inside

That it's time to slide what I adorn most

To the side. Clothes on the floor it's time

To dive, into the ocean where I feel alive.

Because this person I vision with these two

Eyes got my eyes wide open. I then realize

There are words to describe that's unspoken.

The words chosen may come as no surprise.

But by the way you looking,

DECADES

The only thing I feel I can say,

Is My, MY, MY, MY.

Poetic Expressions

LOVE THAT A BLIND MAN
CAN SEE, SHOULD ALSO BE SEEN

"Woman." It's been a long, long time

Coming. But I, prayed to God, not knowing

It would summon your presence.

But You appeared.

Weird how I knew it was you.

One sight, one clue. One life

And it's, with you. I was enrolled

In the wrong program. Therefore

I withdrew. I just knew, the cool in

Me was due to the cool in you.

You're not loving the crew

It's just me. Only time will prove

What I knew would just be.

"Justly." Is how you present

Because you're guided with truth.

DECADES

From start we connected with a

Tight bond, and never decided to

Loose. You're truly something.

I learned if it's meant to be, no

Matter what it's truly coming.

Especially when you're in alignment.

I understood the assignment.

A good thing found

But, how did I find this? I'm

Reminded, that God's favor is granted

Afterwards. Expressing the way I

Feel for you. Even though prior to writing this

I didn't have the words. Just the immense

Feelings. Inevitably the cup ran over.

A situation where I couldn't prevent spilling.

Let's see what our love can do when we constantly

Choose it. Constantly use it for the betterment

Of our Relationship. Loves fully loaded,

So it comes equipped with

DECADES

Everything necessary to make the shift.

It transforms the atmosphere and makes

It feel like Christmas in July. Has Spring

Wondering why its present during winter.

Has me having every reason to believe that I've

Entered into heaven's gates. Because I swear I

Heard the God in Heaven say; "that we have

Arrived." We have survived the worst of the worst.

Kept Love first and can finally rest

Knowing that we have God's best invested in us.

My life is complete. But far from finished.

God said; "You are replenished! She filled the void

You can have hate, but love will destroy."

It's evident, that dreams come true because every

Time I close my eyes, I seem to dream of you.

And then When I wake up, I watch that dream

Transition into Reality. Empowering. Knowing

Instinctually like a bird knows to fly.

That I got you and you got me, a vision I

Will consistently see with eyes open and

EVERY TIME I CLOSE MY EYES.

Poetic Expressions

THE WISDOM OF MAN IS EMBEDDED IN HIS LOVE FOR HER

When a man loves a woman

Try telling that man why he shouldn't.

And he'll tell you exactly why he should.

He loves her, to him, she's everything

And that's exactly why he could.

Even though she bares the potential

To cause extreme misery. When a man

Falls deeply in love it's no mystery. And

There's no real future if you've done wrong

Within the history. Everything she does, he

Finds interesting. Just never betray him.

Cause he'll never betray her. He'll never

Focus on what they say, them, they could

Never display her, within the image that

He sees her. He's only truly happy when

DECADES

He knows that he's pleased her. Her

Satisfaction is what he sees first.

Provider and protector… those are roles

He cherishes. Playboy and unfaithful.

Those roles are roles that perish. Because

When a man loves a woman

He fully upholds commitment

Because a real man fully knows

How to uphold his decision.

It's one that he's made and one that

He will forever stand by. A real man

Can't stand lies. So, he does his best

To never tell them.

When a man loves a woman, his love

Is abundant and comes around way more

Often than seldom. All the promises he makes,

I promise he won't fail them.

And there's no need to ask him why, it's evident,

To him, She's heaven sent. Making everything

Else in the world, just a little less relevant.

Because of HER, to every other woman

He's celibate. Because of HER, he understands

That man finding his woman is the full

Manifestation of our intelligence. Because

Man and Woman carries so much relevance.

And that's what he cherishes and best

Understands. What God hath joined together

Let not man put asunder. A true wonder

In this day and time…. When a man loves

A woman he finds peace. When the love

Is right, every day he finds.

Womanhood is potentially the most

Precious essence of life that life can produce.

Be vulnerable and open with each other

That's how you fight with the truth.

Knockout each other's demons. Every

Man is a shirt, and every woman is the precious

Thread in which it was woven. Every real

Man fully understands the worth of a

MAN LOVING A WOMAN.

Poetic Expressions

SOMETIMES THE RAIN
ARISES WITHIN THE SUNSHINE OF LOVE

On a perfect day our love would

Display all day. The force of

Love would pull us all in and we would

Push away all hate. This sounds all

Great, until a storm arises and causes

All to shake. See we'll for sure break

If we're not grounded. I hope I'm not

Sounding like I'm not with it.

I'm saying I've learned the hard way.

After that I got different. More

Understanding of the demands

Love makes without demanding.

You see I naturally fear,

And want to know for certain

That you are naturally here.

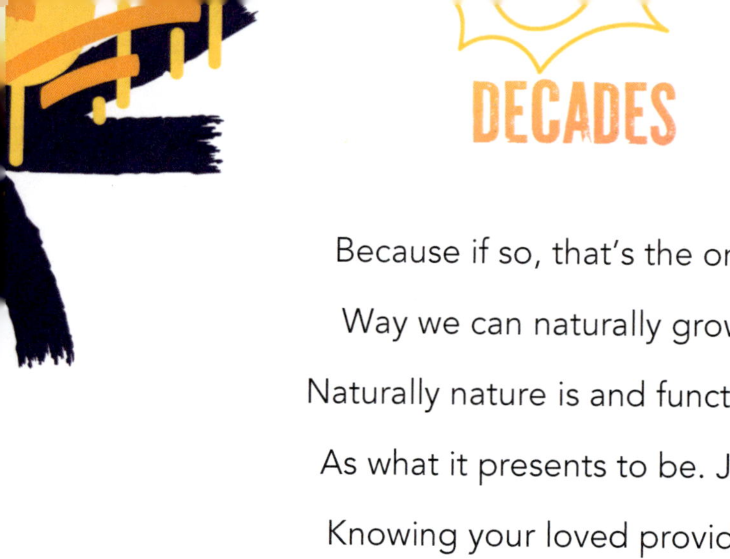

DECADES

Because if so, that's the only

Way we can naturally grow.

Naturally nature is and functions

As what it presents to be. Just

Knowing your loved provides

A natural sense of peace. I wanna

Know for sure that you can strengthen

Me when I present as weak. Please allow

Your heart to unlock when I put in that key.

When you unlock mine, look in and

See. And once you see; if you don't cherish

It please leave it alone. I'll do the same

No need to prolong, that bares the

Potential to bring shame. Pain will

Come no matter what. You opened the

Door to my heart when I had it shut.

When I touch you somehow it still feels

Like I haven't touched. New feelings!

True feelings! Love grew! Then we knew

Healing. Love knew exactly what to do
To pass through ceilings. Elevating
Throughout the galaxy. **True love**
Out powers fallacy. For real for real,
Love is where the power be. How to
Turn sour sweet is similar to how to turn rain
To sunshine. I believe we can make it
Through anything if we operate with
One mind. Make one sound.
Make life great together realizing
We only got one time. One opportunity,
To allow unity to be unison. Perfect
Accord. Parallel to His love for Her
In its truest sense. Your your true
Defense. My love runs deep. Let
Me know if the pressure is too intense.
No pressure though. As time goes
On you learn to understand the pain.
My love, our love is nothing less than

The resemblance of sunshine. If by

Chance clouds emerge and precipitation

Occurs, will the love remain?

When evolution takes over after it demands

A change? Will you be here for me lady?

Will you stand the rain?

Poetic Expressions

THE FIRST TRUE EXPERIENCE
OF LOVE WILL LAST FOREVER

I still remember when I first saw her face.

In me, it immediately imparted faith.

It replaced any feelings I had for any

Other. In that moment I knew I had

Discovered love. I saw a woman in

Her earlier stages of life, which

Made me see an image of the man

I would one day become. Honoring the

Woman I would one day call my wife.

I believed this! They say first impressions

Last forever, that moment allowed me to

See this. Because even to this day your

Love is still remembered as the first.

A curse I swear that I had to move away.

From then I knew the day, would come that

DECADES

I would see you again, you see I had to!

Have you! If I were in my right mind then,

I would have grabbed you and kissed you.

Let you know that I will miss you, immensely;

Intensely; The feelings

I feel lets me know what's meant to be.

We were meant to see, many first times

Together. I still remember the first time we…

Held hands together. Kissed, hugged, made love,

I Mean I loved it. But from the day we separated,

The failure to properly connect has been because of

It. A beauty like yours is part of fate. My

Fate, didn't quite know my flavor back then but

Somehow, I just knew you were my taste.

The average day was the average day.

The days we met again were extravagant.

A reality envisioned that at that time was far

From imagining. Somehow, I remember all this.

Because it was all bliss.

With you, I've never gotten mad.

You know You got it bad. When you've gotten

Sad over the very thought of losing her.

The reason why I can grasp the concept

Of true love to this day, is due to

Her. I'm still true to her, vice versa, she's

True to me. And maybe one day we will

Truly see. The truth that has always stood

Yet lacked the pursuit. There's always a

Lack if the other half of me, isn't you.

Who knows, maybe I'm just stuck in

The past and what I know to be the first sign.

I knew that it was real, a reality I got to feel

For the FIRST TIME.

Poetic Expressions

DECADES

I'M JUST YOURS,
BECAUSE YOUR JUST MINE

I sent a text message to a girl

I used to see, it read I found

A girl whom forever I want to

B with. I hope she C's this and

Finds peace with the decision.

Then I sent a group text to multiple

And declared my division. Really hate to

See her loss, but I'd rather see her winning.

They say don't bring sand to the beach but we

Ain't on the beach, we in the ocean

Swimming. Fully enclosed with love

Like a barrier that allows me to

Keep my distance. For instance;

This one fish, was a blow fish.

She saw me and thought she could

Blow this. Without hesitation I gave

Notice. I got a mermaid, so I don't

Hang with no fish. No dish

Matches my entree. Plus, I was always

Taught to eat what's on plate.

Us right here at this altar is

Beyond fate. Your beyond

Great, I'm honored to be

Amongst your greatness.

I'm prepared to honor this

Commitment no matter what

We're faced with. My homies like;

"A Chris! Reconsider. You can

Get the package but

Say you ain't get the package and

They will re deliver. I'm saying

There's a way you could get more.

Why place one egg in the basket

When you can fit four?" I told him

I traveled that path and she truly

Is the end of this tour. I can't lie

I'll miss that lifestyle but honestly

If I chose it over her, she's the one

I would miss more. I could be piss

Poor and I swear her love would

Make me wealthy. I can do this

Life thing on my own, but I love that

She's here to help me. **Love that**

Grows is love that's healthy. A heart

Once froze, that's now melting. Because

You melt it. I sent you my love, I hope

You felt it. I hope you feel it. As I stand

Here expressing my true feelings. Today

Is only special because we've had true

Dealings. And those dealings are what

Led us here. Staying together is what

Set us clear. Because a clear mindset

Is the only mindset that would get us here.

DECADES

It took time. But in time we were just fine.

Now look, from today and forever on, I'm

Just yours, you're just mine.

Poetic Expressions

IT TOOK REAL LOVE FOR
ME TO REALIZE I HAVE ALL I NEED

All I really need in this life of sin

Is for that one woman to sin with me.

One who can completely

Blend with a bond that mends swiftly.

All I need in this crazy world

Is for a crazy girl to drive me crazy too.

Crazy me, crazy you! Tell me who can

Tame us? A similar answer to the question as

To who tames love? And that answer is nobody!

What's truly amazing is your body,

I can't help but touch.

Similar to lust but much deeper

If lust had a steep slope, the feelings I feel in

Comparison would be much steeper.

If love had a core, we'd be there together.

DECADES

Forever just like love's existence.

Persistence times persistence,

We persist beyond that definition.

Just so happens we exist eternally.

Parallel to eternity our love travels the same

Course. The same force that created us, bonded us

Together. Seems we will never end! Seems We will

Forever spend our existence together.

Sunny days but late nights make the weather

Change. One touch, then a midst, when we began

To kiss, it started to pouring rain. I started storing

Rain collecting its benefits. Giving this everything I

Got because it's our moment. Our time alone in

This dark room. Our sparks boom into fireworks!

Then you become the only person that matters in

This entire earth. My entire search for the right

Woman has ended because you've been found!

The sound of your voice calms the noise inside my

Head. Your love spreads throughout my entirety.

DECADES

I hope my reciprocation does the same for you.

The best recipe for two to breed a third.

My words splurge because loving you is having a

Limitless amount along with everything to

Purchase. **Our surface exists because of things**

Deeper. No reaper to our story, just us leaving this

Space of Life, and entering glory forever and

Always. Hallways, leading to open doors of

Opportunities, possibilities and everything else

Good one could imagine or dream.

It seems as if being with you is a dream,

And it is, but thankfully you also exist in reality!

Go head, Empower me to love you more!

I'll empower you to do the same!

We are to blame Equally.

But who's really blaming who?

Our weakening built our strength!

Our length cannot be measured.

Together is just what we are and since we've

Been That, being severed we disregard!

Because even if Times get hard, we will fight

Harder. We will end up in life martyred if we had

To. Having you I had to, from the moment I saw

You. What to call you, was my first question.

Saying the right thing to steer us in the

Right direction was my first lesson.

"Lucky me" was my first impression.

I'm guessing, being with you is all I see.

Having you and only you to share

This whole Life with, is truly,

All I need!!!!

Poetic Expressions

NO MATTER WHAT YOU CALL HER, SHE IS A NATURAL & ESSENTIAL BEAUTY

She loves me, she loves me not.

A childhood game that, apparently

I've not forgot because even as an adult.

I'm finding myself having to result

To this concept for an answer. She matures,

BEAUTIFULLY, all thanks to the one who

Plants her. Her aroma is as unique as the strains

Of her hairs. The highest of elevation;

I love how she takes me there. There's

Such a connection. No addiction; this

Is a love obsession.

She's only wrong until they say she's not.

Some say she's pot, some say she's weed,

Some say she's gas, some say she's trees.

She's of necessity, every day I need.

DECADES

Every day I plead for forgiveness while

Saying fuck you. I roll my own blunts because

It's always enough to. **A war on drugs, I wonder**

Why she's part of that. War on the drugs

That are artifact. She came from the Earth;

God imparted that. I and those like me thoroughly

Enjoy it. Fuck every salary and hourly employer

That won't employ me because of it.

Me and her are within covenant.

I'm loving this, with her I have a great time.

She sedates minds, helps keep a calm

Composure. I spread her out, then she

Longs for closure. I long to hold her,

I long for her to be closer.

Inhale exhale, take it all in, let it all

Out. She screams in the wind, that's why

She's called loud. I recall sounds, of hatred

Towards her. No matter how many hate her

I will forever adore her. Explore her, different

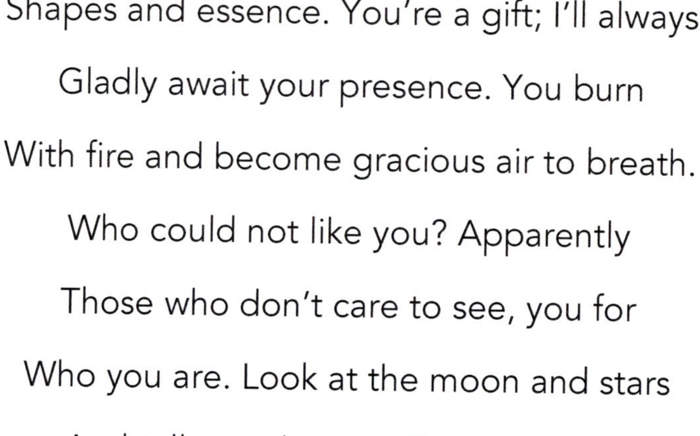

Shapes and essence. You're a gift; I'll always

Gladly await your presence. You burn

With fire and become gracious air to breath.

Who could not like you? Apparently

Those who don't care to see, you for

Who you are. Look at the moon and stars

And tell me what's y'all connection?

I know your good for me because every time

I take you in, I go in an upward direction.

The question? Well it's very simple and

What some may even consider as very plain.

All I request to know, is do you love me?

MARY JANE.

Poetic Expressions

WORDS THAT MATCH
ACTIONS ARE LIKE SCRIPTURES

Girl I'm having a issue. I have a message

And I'm really hoping it gets through.

Coincidently, I only want to send it when I

Get alone with you. You said it

And Mentioned that your love

Carries a particular interest.

Interesting cause you have my

Full attention. And my full interest.

Your four play plays an amazing

And essential role. But can we end it?

So I can lay you down in a proper

Position. Spread your legs, then

Disappear. No fear I'm no magician.

My love wants to combat your love

Just with no opposition. Believe me

DECADES

My love is damn good, just thought

I'd mention. Matter of fact I'll bet that

My love is the best love. **Just feel the**

Way I caress love, inject love inside you

Just to remind you of infinite bliss.

Doesn't get better than this I promise.

Astonished, I bet you will be. I'm well

Aware of the feelings I impute when you

Feel me. And you'll feel me, and the feeling

You'll feel, will be fulfilling. Overly, abundantly

Sync with me, then cum with me. A passionate

Night, it'll all make sense because clearly,

I'm the passionate type. I've had my share

Of lovers. Some say I'm damn good. The

Same will be said by the others. What

Happens under the covers is a wonder

Discovered. So, let's explore better yet

Let's express. Thought you've had good

But the best is yet. To come. I'm not dumb, but

But if you say there's a lesson; I'm willing to learn

Everything your willing to teach. Think you can

Me out. Then prove it and

PRACTICE WHAT YOU PREACH.

Poetic Expressions

WHEN YOU TAKE YOUR TIME, YOU MAKE YOUR TIME

It was 7 O'clock…on the dot…

I thought it was a coincidence.

I was in my ride challenging

The potential of finding my instrument.

Then properly play with it until infinite.

I'm envisioning; this pretty little thang

That's waiting on me. Trying to hastily

Close the distancing. her body called, I answered.

"Increments," of time passed before

We broke past the tension. In my mind I was a

Mathematician. I wanted her legs to

Do division, so I could add to her

Equation. Multiply the sensation then

Multiply the passion. So the

Passion would be aggressive. All this while

Subtracting nothing. My love is

That impressive. I pull up!

Anticipating a great time because

That was objective. Good love! Mind focused

On possession. Planning to exceed what should

Be expected. Then exceed the exceeded expectations

Because I'm That excessive.

I had plans, for my hands to explore

The unexplored parts of her

Moving forward starts with her...

Yes! My favorite are breast. Hands on,

Caress. She liked that, so hands caressed

The rest. Her body was so soft.

The stage was set. So, I showed off.

She put clothes on so I could take

Clothes off. "Patience." First, we rode around

Looking for placement. Then we found the

Destination. Without hesitation, the process

Began quickly. "Desire." The reason I kissed

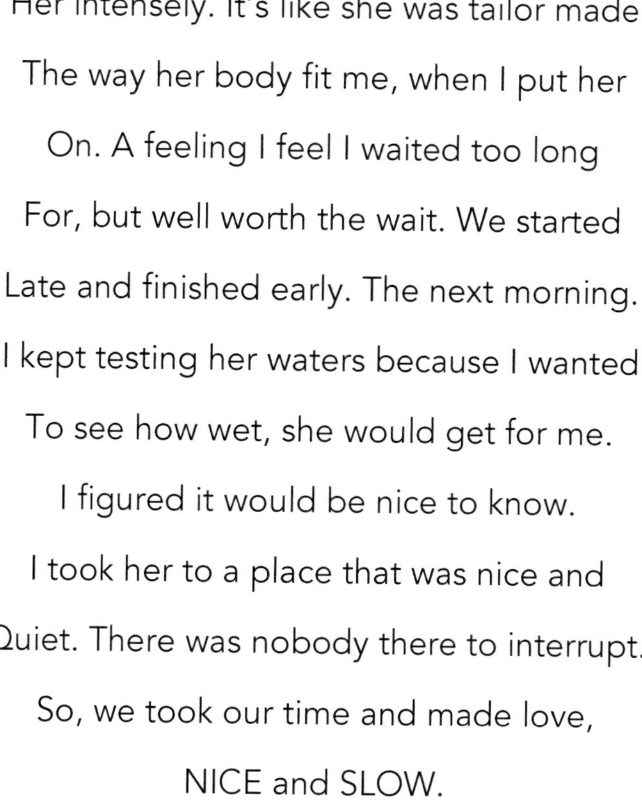

Her intensely. It's like she was tailor made

The way her body fit me, when I put her

On. A feeling I feel I waited too long

For, but well worth the wait. We started

Late and finished early. The next morning.

I kept testing her waters because I wanted

To see how wet, she would get for me.

I figured it would be nice to know.

I took her to a place that was nice and

Quiet. There was nobody there to interrupt.

So, we took our time and made love,

NICE and SLOW.

Poetic Expressions

A LOVE LIKE MINE IS
VERY SIMILAR TO PARADISE

You know dem call me Mr. Bombastic…

Fantastic!

Make that pum pum drip like faucet!

A female lover lover!

A wonder discovered, once

Discovered. Once I take you under

You'll love it there. Introduction

To ecstasy. Unaware that you

Could feel this great. She said

I'm fantastic. Quite supreme!

She said she was fully awake in

The bed but, the love we made was quite

The dream. I told her I like to bring,

Pleasure to excite some things.

Be the cause of that very mess

DECADES

Just so afterwards I can wipe it clean.

Sexual, that provides true healing.

Having riddim when you grind

Inserts new feelings, each and every time

I can promise you that.

I don't require a map to navigate your body.

Nice and naughty, that's how you

Like it probably. When we finish, this bed

Will be nice and sloppy. What I produce you'll

Want Me to display. Just lay,

I'll take it from there. Let's move like ocean.

With the backdrop of ocean.

Sharing in moments of Passion. Mr. Romantic!

You'll love me if you love Romancing.

Heart panting, breath baby!

I'll take it easy. Pleasure because

I make it pleasing. I'll make that body go boom!

Once More, then we'll make it even

I love within that's the major reason.

I'm only slowing down so we can pace

The breathing. I'm slowing down

So I can supply this force. Slow wine that

Body. Because I truly believe wine is meant to

Be paired with the finest course!

Mr. Luva luva. A real man

In these streets. A real beast under the covers.

What I do to you, will make you wanna tell

Others. **Way better than your rose! Because**

I rise! A real treat to that beautiful cake

Between thy thighs. Can slip the rubber

On but it's not rubber made or plastic.

You want love that far exceeds your

Previous experiences and expectations

Then you want me…. Mr. BOOMBASTIC

Poetic Expressions

A SOFT REQUEST
SPEAKS LOUD & CLEAR

First let me say I'm a nasty man. You allowing me

Past these pants will introduce pleasures that you

Will never experience without this

Chance. These hands are meant to

Caress you. This tongue is meant to

Lick that clit. And those breasts too.

You match with me, then you've met

Your match. I'm here to bring out the

Best you. Yes you, can cream on my

Face. When I like it, I lick it clean,

Especially when clean is the taste.

You want it faster, slower, or

Are you loving this pace? Welcome

To my sex room, where creating

Pleasure is the only use for this space.

DECADES

Kiss me. Lick me. When I erupt,

Erupt with me. Touch me. Suck me. After

That I'll lick you till your soaking wet.

Then beat it up abruptly. Intense huh?

That's the way it's supposed to be.

You've had good…supposedly. I

Understand good is good until you've

Gotten a hold of me. I'll show you superior.

Believe me when I get within, I naturally

Get a feel for how to properly stroke the interior.

With every stroke's intent, to make

You go to a stage of ecstasy you've never

Went. This will be the best time you've

Ever spent. I can do this for hours and hours

Because I truly like to feel pussy. No, I'm not

A killer. But upon request I do kill pussy.

But not with deadly force.

I prep before the assassination

That's where the head resorts. Not eating

Pussy comes from the dead beats course.

I can't be no dead-beat no. I put HE (meaning

Boat) in your river. Then I let HE row.

I know you want it. Just let me know.

From there you'll see, you've never

Experienced feelings quite like this.

Just wait till you see my dick.

Poetic Expressions

HER WETNESS IS A
POOL THAT I LOVE TO DIVE IN

See the lust in your eyes, is so

Evident. You provide the best feeling

In the present tense. That grip while

Inside, that slip when I slide. First I

Dip, then I dive. I strive to keep you

Cummin over and over. That cum comes

Closer and closer the more I stroke.

The longer I stay in it, the more I know.

I wanna know you best. Suck me first,

I'll lick next. See, I'm a passionate lover

I love passionate sex. I love when passion

Connects. That's when it becomes better

Than as good as it gets. Your so juicy

For me. I'm good and horny. Rain rain

Don't go away. It's actually good you're storming.

DECADES

Shit let it storm some more.

Battle of the sexes, our pursuit to

Please each other turns to war.

We fight until it's night night.

Chocolate dipped in cream.

A description of what's in my sight.

What I like, is her juices spilling down my pipe.

It feels best when she's my type. "Eyesight"

Is important but I want you to close your eyes

And focus. Talk is cheap but I speak with boldness.

My talk is deep, and it's only provided

When actions are guaranteed motions.

Oceans are great to swim in, but swimming

In your waters is my favorite. It's a joy

Like obtaining what you desired because

God favored it. I love a freak who sucks

After I stick it in because she likes flavored

Dick. Started with a starting five up until

You became my favorite pick. I lick

Just to get her started. When she moves

And moans that's when my dick hardens.

I make the beat, it's on track, she screams

Notes that sounds like a melody.

Body keep talking, I'm paying close attention

And listening to everything she's telling me.

Sometimes I wonder if I should stop.

But then those drops start compelling me.

That feeling too. Bare no shame while

You naked let this ecstasy start revealing

You. Plus I'm always delighted when

You open up and introduce me.

Ooh that pussy is wet, but I bet, I

Can make it JUICY.

Poetic Expressions

WE BECOME EMBEDDED IN
UNISON WHEN YOU BECOME ME AND I YOU

"Assimilation!" Suddenly I'm feeling

What you feeling, while the feelings

Accumulating. "Reciprocation."

I'm giving what you giving. Swimming

With no vision. Just following the

Feeling from the precipitation.

"Patience." I can't wait but will,

If I have to end up waiting.

Eye contact to match the intensity.

I made her soul leave her body,

Then get into me. As I feel

Her leave, I'm staying inside.

My hands on her chest, I can feel the beat

While I'm pumping. She's staying alive!

1 season of Love has led to series. Loves in the air

DECADES

That's clearly! Loves' screaming. I love bringing,

Her to the place a place of climax.

We're like high hats, two cymbals symbolizing

Love on a stand with the pedal to the metal.

Such a beautiful sound when I tap.

A beautiful clash each time I slap.

We're only here to please. No hesitation, heavily

I hear her breath. I went inside to make

Her go. From the outside I could hear her

Leave. I feel her flow. I feel her needs

I feel her desires for pure passion.

The buildup of it all was suspenseful,

But now it's pure action.

Our love is tailor made like top tier fashion.

I'm "Prada" (proud of) her, so elated

For me she opened "Dior" (The door). So

I could swim in her until the tide leads

Me back to the seashore. I be here baby!

You see me your man, I see you my

Lady. When I see you I'm craving…

Intimacy with you because I know

Once we're intimate, we'll be here feeling

Amazing. You don't have to say, not

One word. The connection we have speaks

For itself. **The communication is often**

Unheard, but always felt. "Synergy."

Doesn't quite make sense but

We successfully produce through

Positive and creative energy. I see you

Baby! I pay attention to what I see in you

Daily. We touch then you take me,

To a place where you give and I give

No one's taking. Love were making.

It makes sense. Quite intelligent

The way I please you. Although pleasing you

Doesn't take sense. It takes connection, Intuition,

And a great perception. To properly follow

It takes direction. To properly lead you must

Know your path and follow it with no

Exceptions. I know your questions

I have your answers. In no way shape or

Form am I insinuating that your see through

Lady. I know all that I know because I be

you baby. I BE YOU baby.

Poetic Expressions

DECADES

SOME PEOPLE WANT LOVE, I NEED IT

When I'm alone in my room, sometimes I stare at

My door. Really wishing that walking through

Once more, will be you **The thought occurred in**

my mind that I need true Love and a good woman

I must find. I can't forever be blind to these facts.

The multiple mishaps I've had with Love

Came from me playing games with many hearts.

Creating many sparks leading them to believe that

Flames of love would burst soon after.

We shared lots of good times with laughter,

Yet when true commitment was demanded,

Things would change. And I would never allow

Those sparks to burst into Flames. The truth hurts

So, I played games, watered down truth, and left

You hurt and alone. I now realize that I'm wrong

So tears start to flow from my eyes. Because I

Realize that you are a Dove! So sweet, so gentle,

Sent from above! And I'm so unworthy of your

Touch, let alone your Heart. One part of me

deserve to be alone, deferred from the world,

Just void. But the other part, because of you, makes

Me feel like I'm worthy of the love, warmth and

Affection that is created by a girl and a boy.

"I NEED LOVE"

How sweet it must be, to have a woman in my life

To make my life complete. I wanna find the type

Of woman who can bring life to me. My wife to be,

The type I see when I close my eyes to imagine.

A wonderful thought and sight to fathom, but I

Would much rather be having you by my side.

The type of woman who will be Bonnie to this

Clyde; Or simply put my ride or die. So, it's no

Wonder why I constantly Love you without

Stopping. Anything you tell me about yourself, I'm

DECADES

Jotting it down because I care about every fact

Concerning you. You Are my wish come true,

My very heart's beat. **If you were cold**

I would be your heat, if you were falling,

I would be Your crane! I know you are tired of

Being hurt So please Allow me to be your change.

I wanna estrange you

From the pains you've felt from your past lovers.

Allow my love, in a very real way, blow their

Mistakes right up under the covers

Leaving them to disappear like a magician.

Let my real Love partition you from the fake.

Can't shake, break or tarnish what we have, I grasp

At every breath, that I get with you.

But where are you at?

You got me searching here and there, I swear

I'm simply yearning true love, or should I say, I'm

Simply yearning you… LOVE! Desperately

Searching like a fiend, if you know who you are;

DECADES

Stand up, jump around, speak aloud, please just

Simply make Yourself seen. Take this chance in

Love with me, and I promise you will know just

What I mean. I'm a good man, I promise to be

Honest and true. Making you my bride when I find

You, I will always remind You of my love.

I will go above and beyond!

I will do, I won't just try.

Because when I finally find you, I will take heed

To that opportunity and I promise,

I will pour all of my love inside.

"I NEED LOVE"

I just wanna kiss and hold you, help mold you

To become the woman your called to be.

I'll help carry that vision; I'll see to it that you live

Your best life. Be the best wife, as I vow

To be the best husband. Always providing good

Loving. Because having such a good woman

Provides fuel to our moments of ecstasy. Never go

Away, Never leave me alone, I always want you

Next to me. However, if we ever have to be apart.

Let's be sure to converse via video messaging or

Over the phone. The sound of your voice is my

Favorite tone and conversations with you, creates

My favorite songs. "SWV I'm weak," my heart

Skips beats when Your next to me. I crave the

Whole you, because the whole you, brings out the

Best in me. You mean so much to me from the

Inside out. **I'll shout my love for you on mountain**

Tops, make mountains drop, if they are ever too

High for you to reach me. I hope you hear it in my

Voice how badly I need thee O' Love. I hope to rise

Above my desires for a love brought to fruition.

But how can I find you? Learn more about you?

I'm willing to pay whatever tuition

To be able to learn your curriculum.

No core classes, I'm skipping them.

Because my major concern is to learn,

DECADES

More about you, just sign me up for

Classes right now, because, I can't take another

Day Without you. I often fantasize about a time

That you and I can share. Me pulling your hair

Grabbing your neck. Rubbing your body, it's so soft

Your so wet, and I love how you feel. You got me

Hard As steel. I peel your panties back. Our bodies

Get closer and interact, we break into heavy

Breathing, then heavily we begin to sweat.

Although this is only a fantasy,

I know it will become real. It just hasn't yet.

But when it does, I know we will create

An experience that I will never forget.

"I NEED LOVE."

Because of you I've changed. I grew up and

Stopped playing games. Exchanged them

For true manhood, always respecting, honoring

And cherishing a real woman, just like a

Man should on the daily.

DECADES

Some may call me crazy because that's the way I

Want to do things for the rest of my life. Finally

Realizing that I will never become the King

I'm destined to be, without my Queen also known

As, my wife. Life is not the same without you.

I'll never doubt you could have found someone

Else. But I will doubt you would have found the

Level of Love that only comes from a man such as

Myself. I can't help but to be braggadocios.

Only placing my Focus on being your man.

Understand that I will take heed to your ways and

The words you speak. **My love for you will go**

Clouds high and oceans deep. I'll reach either

Depth if either brings me one more step closer to

Finding you. If not, then I guess

I'll continue trying to. Because I can't sit back

And wait for my Queen and me to meet.

I gotta compete with these other fools who will

Attempt to seek your love, only to fail because

I'll be struggling and fighting the with forces of

Hell only to prevail and find you. So that I can

Remind you that you, are my girl! And when I

Finally do, just watch how our love Unfurls.

"I NEED LOVE."

You see, as I'm sitting here alone in my room

Staring at the door. I'm fantasizing about

The day that door will open. Still hoping

And believing in the day when you come

Home where you belong. **I now know that I need**

True Love, and with it I can't go wrong. I just need

You to be willing to make yourself seen so like I

Have all the time in the world, I'll be sitting here

Waiting, proving my love and desire for you.

Know that I adore you and I'll become a better

Man because of you. I'll be waiting. I LOVE You!

Poetic Expressions

LIFE DESIRES BECOME
LIFE CONSEQUENCES, CHOOSE WISELY

"Redundant." repetition doesn't always

Produce abundance; I've yet to strike gold

Within these rivers I consistently wash my

Hands in. Although I still have hope that

With these waters I can win; I have to face

That at this moment the depth is too deep

For me to stand in. I can swim but right

Now I find Myself drowning

Alarm sounding and I hear it.

But instead of running away, I ran near it.

Can you hear this? At one point I stood fearless

And confident. Not realizing my incompetence

To choose the path I had chosen. Was in too

Much of a mindset to be a man molded.

In an image, that I never myself molded.

I fell victim to the fear of life. I crawled

Up but now I stand firm and unfolded.

See I thought I knew what I

Was doing, and what I wanted. **But, Only**

When you mature, are you haunted by your

Days of immaturity. An impure purity. Are you

Sure it's me? Because I wouldn't have done that,

But I did it. All in the name of love I got

Over committed and lost myself in the process.

You can look at life like a project. Still be careful

Of the Experiments. Know that everything

Carries its own experience.

And every experience carries its own lessons.

Every deposit ain't an investment. Everyone you

Choose to be in love with don't add, sometimes

They lessen. luckily for me, a couple of those curses

Turned out blessings. Because all things work together

For the good of those….I been through the dirt, I

Got out because I knew that from out of it I could

DECADES

Of Rose. (*"The Rose From The Concrete"* reference; *Tupac Shakur*)

Different path for my life I could of chose.

But would that mean that I wouldn't have the

Same reality? Totality reflects what actually

Is. What I actually did cannot be done

Differently. In this case, different is a fantasy.

Will never get the chance to play situations back,

The hand you deal is the only hand you see.

If I hand you me, please take care of me.

Because I've seen how I give myself non sparingly.

And most times that means I end up used, lost and

Very confused. I got pushed out into this world

Thinking Like a man but I was still an adolescent.

I had a question or two, or three, or maybe more!

But who stops to think of a reason that

Superman would need saving for?

And who stops to ask questions when they swear

They know the answer?

DECADES

Life can seem like cancer. **And people can**

Seem like cancer cells, the more evil excels

The more cells it turns cancerous. Multiple

Questions that need answering. I feel the

Questions will never cease. Please

Understand life's disease is

Not benign. And we're not designed to destroy

It or make it worse. I can't disperse on empty.

Understand that pain gets worse when there's

Plenty. Figure it out, that's what I'm trying to do.

But it truly takes time before you find your

Truth. And when you do, it takes even more

Time to filter the pain out from all the lies.

A reality once lived, that was all disguise. Pure

Intentions and pure hope. Now I got a clear

Scope to live free and lonely. Time heals

All, so as Time passes, please go

EASY ON ME.

Poetic Expressions

DECADES

LOVE SHOWN IN THE LIGHT
CAN ALSO BECOME A SHADOW

I'm out of shape, currently unfit to do

What it takes to make a relationship

All that takin trips and buying gifts,

So sorry! Not sorry! But I ain't on that shit!

And it's mostly because I had bad ones

So, I can never again get on that trip.

A trip, huh? how the good guys get turned bad.

Mad at the world for our mistreatment.

It's like I was stuck in a constant cycle of

Heart given, then heart beaten.

My heart's weakened, falling in love is

Now a pretense. Don't want to get hurt

Again, so I prevent the opportunity.

No time for unity, no time for you and me.

I took that class, now it's met with my truancy.

DECADES

My heart was real open until over and over it got

Shut. Now ask me how many times that door

Opens, and I'll tell you "not much."

Shit not at all. Sometimes you gotta fall,

Reassess then get back up

And face those uncertainties.

I've just concluded love don't work for me.

And even if it does, I'm far too traumatized

To let it. The moment my heart gets involved

I seem to be manic. I panic when she's away

From me, triggered by things she may say to me.

I mean I truly feel wronged when she

Doesn't answer that phone while she's out.

Not sure what that's all about.

I figure it's too hard to understand

So my resolve is just to miss out completely.

I try to combat the negative thoughts

In my head but they always seem to defeat

Me. Don't know if I'm right or wrong about

DECADES

What I'm thinking, but I'll keep thinking

It until the opposite is factual. My actual

Heart fades when it feels played or

Misused. If confused, I ask questions.

The answers given, I learn lessons and

Make the determination of whether I leave

Or stay. Constantly maintaining my own

Lawn, trying to keep the weeds away.

I smoked weed today and I'll smoke

It again tomorrow. Trying to rid my

Sorrow by staying high. **Trying to fly**

With no wings not realizing I'm risking

My life jumping off these cliffs. Wondering

Why all these rifts keep occurring.

Maybe I'm stirring pots that don't need

Stirring, or maybe I'm worrying about all

The wrong details. Fucked up in the head,

Not sure if there's a woman who can prevail

The thoughts that I'm constantly contemplating

With. And for that reason, amongst others

I'd much rather we kick it strictly, on the

LATE NIGHT TIP.

Poetic Expressions

PRAY FOR THOSE WHOM YOU'VE HURT, THEN LEARN TO HURT NO MORE

Thou shalt not break yo heart.

Thou shalt not take your start

Then, blindly drag you to the finish line.

Thou shalt replenish time, if it's time

You wasted. Thou shalt hear the truth

Because it's time you face it! How do

You replace a one of a kind? For that

You cannot obtain replacement. How

Are you not adjacent? Right here is where

You need to be. Right here is where you

Were before I introduced reason for

You not to believe in me! "What could

The reason be?" A good thing you asked!

The reason is I failed to stand on what I

Promised. And within a moment I let you

DECADES

Pass. I left you mad after making you

Happy. What I did to make you sad

You would have never done to me gladly.

Subtracting, because I know I added nothing.

Thou shalt not claim full house when

He knows he's bluffing. Thou shalt

Call it what it is instead of having

It exposed as nothing, or something,

Other than What thou said it was.

Thou shalt align his actions

With exactly what thou says he does!

I said it cause I meant it. Then I said

And did things that went against it.

Now, I'm down on my knees, because I

Cannot stand distance. From

You! We're two when we should

Be one. This is like a dark moon.

With you it was a bright sun.

A foolish man I am! Thinking like

DECADES

A man who can, but just because

You can doesn't mean that you have to.

You ain't moving careful if moving too fast.

You know its many things out here ready to

Trap you. The likes of you.

While it may not be easy, sometimes

You gotta do what you gotta do

And that ain't always what you like to do.

I realize it now. Hate that it came

At the expense of losing you after doing

Things wrong. When all along, all this

Could have been avoided had I simply

Chosen to do what I knew was right to do!

Thou shalt partake; in everything good,

Never anything that leads to heartbreak.

Or heartache. If I start late, will that mean

We gotta finish early? Matter of fact,

Go ahead, be done with me.

You deserve to be finished hurting.

Cause I ain't even worthy, or

Deserving of another chance to become

Another version. I could have been

That originally. Physically you were

Never abused but, those emotions

Are so scarred. I tried so hard to

Never hurt you. Only to choose

Moments where I'd desert you. Lord

Dry these tears as I peel these layers.

Don't let her heart mourn the hurts

I caused. Lord be her savior. Please

Give her one more chance at love

And may that love be much greater.

On my knees I pray, asking Lord please!

Answer, this PLAYER'S PRAYER.

Poetic Expressions

IF YOU'RE NOT CAREFUL, LOVE GAINED CAN BECOME LOVE LOST

"Reminiscing." I still remember

The times we were together.

So hard to fathom the fact that we're

Apart. I know the mission was for

Us to be forever, somehow the

Mission failed and I'm left with

A broken heart. The parts that

Play fondly in my mind are all

The times you were intimately mine.

And I yours. My mind wars with

The acceptance of losing you.

Our love stayed put until I

Started moving you. You were

First place but got moved to two.

My mistake! When you think it's abundant

DECADES

You fail to realize times at stake.

Made love then! We were happy there!

I wonder if I seek hard enough

Can I once again find that place?

The value of your love was perpetually high.

Not sure why, I discounted you.

I hate you left me, but I also realize

I'm accountable. I didn't love you like

I could, if given another chance I would.

Even back then I knew I should,

But I couldn't. My heart told me it

Was ok to love, but my mind wouldn't.

Allow me to leave the past in the past.

I trashed what was never disposable.

Now my life is fading, because

I can't last without holding you.

I can't eat because without

You I'd rather starve, I can't sleep

Because it's too hard to sleep alone.

DECADES

What do you do when you constantly

Seek to obtain what's permanently gone?

What's wrong? Better yet what's right?

What's life if you aren't living?

Your love found me when the

Love in my heart was distant.

Before I ever faced heartbreak I

Loved different. Gave the best parts

To ones that were unworthy. Then I met

You, and I stopped hurting. And

Then I treated you similar to how

I was once treated. I allowed a cycle

To be repeated in Vice versa. Despite

The version of myself that you saw.

Not loving you correctly is my true flaw.

I failed to evolve into the man I

Needed to be. See, for so long I

Had it wrong. You made my house

My home. Now I'm lost in this world

DECADES

Like a vagabond.

Right now, I feel compelled to die.

When you left, you took the wind

Beneath my wings, then I fell from sky.

And I'm still fallin. No signal but I'm

Still callin. S.O.S. I left you with

No choice but to save yourself.

I left a mess! And I honestly can't

Deal with the mess I made myself.

I need help! And you were the one

That helped. The numbness overcomes

Because you were the only one I felt.

I wish I could get you to understand

What I understand and see much clearer.

See, today I see a Better man

When I look at the man in the mirror.

But it's too late. I was too wrong

To someone who to me, was too great.

Tell me what do you do when the one you need,

No longer needs you? For me; it's making me

Bleed, with no heart to bleed through.

I'm lifeless, knowing I can't turn you

On because you turned off. Yet, I

Still yearn so desperately for this love,

That's now lost. LOVE LOST

Poetic Expressions

SELF REFLECTION IS THE
BEST REFLECTION TO GIVE TO SELF

Man in the mirror. I hope you

See life clearer now. Got some

Cuts and bruises I see. It's

Harder than ever for on your face to

Appear a smile.

Made some bad calls in life. You need

A clearer dial. They

Appeared as foul, clearly you

Have discernment. God gave

You life with honor and favor.

But you can dis earn it. Lucky

Candles burning. Turning to

Luck for faith. Outward representations

Are just that. You only understand

What you see when you look within.

DECADES

**Everything starts within, then transforms

Towards an outward break.** You have

Outwards hate, some of it stems within.

The love inside you combats

That external hate, I hope you know

Who's bound to win. You found the sin,

Upon conception. You learned to access

It once you found deception. "Exceptions."

I don't believe there are any in the eyes

Of God. He who understands replies with

Nod. Need I say more? Only you can

Determine how great your life will be.

Clear those bumps before you bring

That face forward. Mature more.

Really understand what you're good for.

You can claim a stance of ten toes,

But many foes will come along to sway

You. Believe me; Evil is cunning and always

Bares the potential to fold those who

DECADES

In all aspects don't display truth. Only
Display youth while you're young. **Be
Present in your own time of existence.
And maybe you'll exist more.** Know
Exactly what you exist for. Know exactly
Why you appreciate it. Then strengthen
This core. If the core is weak, you're not
Centered. Without balance you can not
Enter. A realm where peace is a devout
Winner in every fight against it. **Want this
World to change be the change against
It.** Know how to move though. With
Wisdom is the best way to move bro.
Life ain't easy. Sometimes things get hot.
That's when it's best to think that it
Can get cool though. When it gets
Cold, know that it can get warm. Duality
Is an inevitable work in this life, you
Have been warned. I have been torn,

But I believe I'm back together almost

Totally. I realize every decision made

Has percentage of the total me. Trying

To get a hold of me when sometimes

I'm too weak to carry me. Add to this life

Then you owe those lives proper parenting.

Everyday my mind works on becoming a

Better father. A better man. Not seeking

To be better than, just a representation

For better man. Hoping better can bring

Better forth. Love is a better force.

And a better course. Clear the path,

See the path clearer. I'm gonna make

A change. And it starts with this

MAN IN THE MIRROR

Poetic Expressions

LIFE CREATES MOMENTS YOU OVERLOOK, ONLY TO ONE DAY CHERISH

Sometimes I wish I could return

To the day where the pressure was lighter.

Then again, "heavy is the crown." I must

Remember I'm a fighter. Just the part in me

That won't allow me to give in to that.

Grandpa told me to be your own man.

You follow if you in the midst or in the back.

You lead being in the forefront. If

You want others to follow, mend the track.

But always lead the way. I remember the days.

When Grandpa was here to talk to me.

I wish I could have those days back, because

The present seems off to me. Nonetheless,

On my way I go. No matter how many set

Backs life presents, forward movement will

DECADES

Forever be the only way I know. At least I hope

Because I'm not immune to falling prey to

Weakness's predatory ways. I remember

Plays being made when I wasn't even playing.

I remember saying I was saved without

Knowing what I was saying. Now I'm wiser

And move to a different beat. Yet everyday

I'm still praying. Cause I still believe just,

Not how they believe it. I have reason to

Believe what I believe for my reasons.

My seasons have given me flavor. Along

With moments I will never cherish. I thank God

For the moments I can savor. I remember

Fishing. And that the more weight you added

On the line, furthered your depth and distance.

Sometimes I have visions, of life being

Lived much better than how I'm currently

Living. I'll get there! I swear! Forget if

They don't. I care! I pair well only with

DECADES

My destiny. I remember days when I was

Much happier. I'm working real hard for

Those days to stick with me. I remember

Family time and how special it meant to

Me. I hate how the losses within family

Still gets to me. I learned the hard way

That thinking you have all the time in the

World is trickery. A real mystery what the

Future holds. I really wish the future wasn't

So mysterious. Cause I'm real curious

About what the future knows. Although

I'm still trying to balance out what the past

Means. God awoke me to show me that I have

Dreams. That I slept on. And that slumber I must

Come out of. Then He reminded me of all that He's

Done for me, and all that He's brought me

Through, and all of this...became NOSTALGIA

Poetic Expressions

GEORGIA'S POEM;
WHERE A BOY BECAME A MAN

I was born in San Diego California but raised

In Georgia. Home of the Braves! Here

You learn to keep a track record of standing

Up towards everything that comes towards ya.

You can be afraid, so long as you know fear

Won't save you. Face that fear because

Being brave is what makes you. Round these parts.

Every town bares its own essence.

My presence here began in Norcross.

The swiftly to the Mountain we went.

Back then I can't lie, I couldn't understand why we

Left those palm trees and ocean views.

But now I see momma did what momma had to

Do. This must be fate. I remember sitting in the

Classroom amongst my classmates. Thinking to

Myself; I'm where I'm supposed to be. Feels like

Home away from home. A place that would

Become well known over the years. I learned a lot

From peers. I got tears that fell on these soils.

Happy I no longer toil with many of the

Reasons that Made those tears fall.

At some point I realized I Veered off track

When I sat down, from that point on I stood tall!

"I can make life ALLGOOD, if within my

Choices I choose my FREEDOM." They

Chose to try to defeat me, I chose to

Beat them. They chose to use and abuse me.

I chose to never need them. Now they have

To see me shine! While I choose to never

See them. Oh Georgia! A supporter for

Most of what I've been through!

Can't say it's been all bad though.

Some people have become like family.

Some I will never be kin to. If anyone

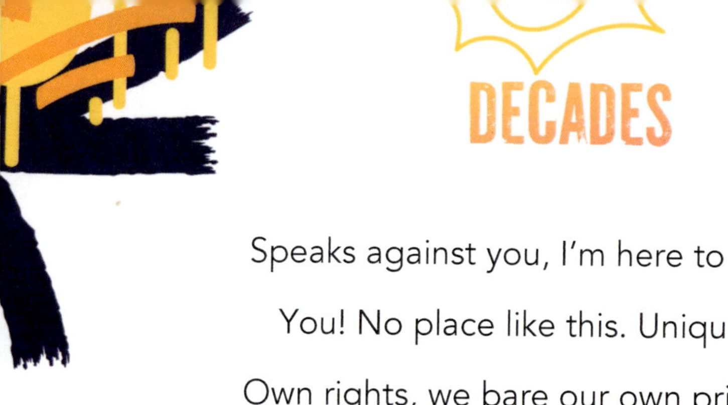

DECADES

Speaks against you, I'm here to defend

You! No place like this. Unique in it

Own rights, we bare our own principles.

It's understood if you're a man of that manner.

You can be raised outside of it and still know the

Heartbeat of this whole space is Atlanta!.

Great when we come together. Hate when

We fall apart! Take the love it's better,

Hate the hate that attempts to steal your

Heart. Be part of what's greater, because

That's what will forever remain. One day

Love will come to take with and sweep away

Whatever remains. Pains will exist no longer.

All who go will all be stronger. Representative

Of your good or bad works. It's important to

Know that good heals, bad hurts. In Georgia,

I've come across good and bad. Overall

What this land has to offer I believe is purity.

A heartfelt connection with the essence of

Southern hospitality. I wasn't born here, I

Was raised here, therefore I faced this reality.

And what it showed me is; opportunity,

Possibilities, culture, unity, most of all

It showed me community. And how we

Ride for ours. On 20 I can ride for hours.

And whether I ride to another state, you can await,

Cause one day, I'll be heading back towards ya!

Because your always on my mind… Georgia!

Poetic Expressions

WHEN LOVE IS TRUE, IT BECOMES AS SWEET AS A TRUE LOVE SYMPHONY

Is it true love if it's only shown

When you declare it? Who can

Tell you how long to bare the pain

When you're the only one who has to bare it?

If we share it, guaranteed it's based on

Our own merit. If someone shows you hate,

How dare they care if you become careless?

I seek peace but sometimes I wonder

What If I'm seeking wrong. Somebody find

The love in my heart, I think it's gone.

Gone with the wind. Life ain't going your

Way take a long look within. And I swear

There will be an answer. You took my

Grandparents, I won't dare make

Peace with cancer. It lurks in the night,

DECADES

But I promise you won't dare defeat this panther.

Is it, real love if you don't feel loved?

Lord why do I feel this way?

Why do I do what I'm supposed to do

And I still get played?

Why is this world filled with hatred?

Why do we quote your laws and then

Disgrace it? By the time one became worthy

Of my heart, I noticed I misplaced it.

Ain't this how it always goes?

I wanna leave this classroom but they

Say the hallways closed. Lockdown!

Gotta learn this lesson to earn progression.

When I do that's when I'll be able to say

I can't be stopped now.

Lord How do I grow perfectly?

I mean is there even such a thing?

Please heaven put out a search for me.

And when you find me, wipe me clean.

DECADES

You designed me to put in work for thee.

Yet I find myself in search for means.

How do I walk when filled with uncertainty?

Is my reality what it seems?

Are my dreams meant to be fulfilled?

Are my goals meant to be met?

When they are what do I do from there?

Once fulfilled will I forget?

The very reason I wanted to fulfill them.

Am I only asking because I haven't yet?

Trying to find reason to never try.

Let my children breathing always be the reason

Why. Why I became who I was supposed to.

Can't run away if God chose you.

I hate I have so many questions.

Life can become quite confusing.

Lawless people living lawlessly.

But I have faith and hope in this conclusion.

All things work for the good of those…

DECADES

And **True love resides in the hearts**

Of those who choose to choose it!

Poetic Expressions

THERE IS GLORY IN FINDING YOURSELF, THERE IS VICTORY IN FULFILLING YOUR PURPOSE

I'm not asking for your love, that's not why

I make my poetry. I owe myself, I told myself

I can't keep ignoring the gift that's within me.

I can't keep falling prey to the temptations that

Tempt me taking me away from fulfilling my

Vision. I can't just mention what I wanna do.

I gotta let my actions speak louder than my words

For that's the only way I'm gonna prove that I can.

The manner of man that I am, makes me rather

Suffer alone, than to allow someone the

Opportunity to refuse their help. Placing me

In a position to conclude myself, as the only one

Responsible for any failure. Causing me to grind

Until the things I grind to obtain become familiar.

And from there I hope to inspire the masses.

With no need for matched to light this fire.

The friction between my opposition and my

Desires creates this combustion! Which leads to the

Consumption of my opposition. Allowing it to be

The addition to the fire of my desires which shall

Be forever lit, Ima forever run this marathon.

I'll never quit. Until my time's up. Hoping to

Inspire the world to incline love to its proper

Heights. Giving it proper rights and proper

Placement, proper intaking and distribution. No

More confusion, Love is not to blame! **Love is not**

The game, It's the cheat sheet! Being the very

Reason why you And I, can advance through all

Levels of life, without having to repeat any levels.

Love is within the dust and is still there

When the dust settles, **Love is infamous! Love can**

Be felt in increments, found at levels that's infinite;

DECADES

Love is energy, love is thought, love is free,

It can't be bought. It can be sought and it

Can be found. Love is around even when you

Believe it's not. **Love is omnipresent,** within us all,

There's not a spot on earth that can deny its

Presence. Not a human alive that can deny its

Essence. We all know love, we just choose hate.

We just choose fate for evil to remain relevant.

We enlarge hell, for the hell of it. Let's choose to

Stop. Let's choose to watch the examples before us

And walk their paths in the sand placing a demand

On change because it's all evolution.

Were all the solution to the problems that exist.

Gods and goddess, lets choose to be more God like.

Represent God right. Because He gave us an image

In His likeness, and as I write this; I hear God

Speaking, telling me to strengthen His people, not

Weaken. Become a beacon of hope and a ray of

Light. Fix my sight on the things above knowing

Everything else will fall in place. Rest well Ermias.

Thank you for exposing us to the Marathon

We all race to finish. No time for split decisions

We gotta set our minds to love and embrace the

Change. Because that grants us all range to

Connect. Interject our greatness, establish our

Placement in this race we're racing. Making tonight

Our night, and this our very moment!

Feel good about living this life! Keep going!

Your decisions, please own them.
And lets make history.

Finishing our individual races within this life,
with Victory!

www.ingramcontent.com/pod-product-compliance
Lightning Source LLC
Chambersburg PA
CBRC100839110726
48006CB00013B/1450